MW00715951

THINK WEALTHY

Top 10 Ways to Train Your Brain for Financial Success

CONTENTS

OUR ONLY FINANCIAL JOB IN LIFE

Our only financial job in life is to pay our monthly bills until game over.

That's it.

Even billionaires have monthly bills – and lots of them!

How do we pay our monthly bills after schooling ends, on through our years in the workforce and all the way through what might be decades of retirement?

If you've got that all figured out, then this book series will keep you "in the conversation" and motivated toward financial independence and/or more wealth creation.

For most people reading these books, however, you were raised in families that approached this financial job of ours by thinking about it month-to-month – I JUST clear the hurdle of affording one month before I start planning (and worrying) about the next month – which is a very middle class approach – and which is fine if that's all you've ever known like me.

The KEY to successful personal finance, however, is to learn to think and to plan year-to-year, to have a longer time horizon in mind. To do that is to Think Wealthy, which is the sole purpose of the words I'm stacking next to each other in all the books in this series.

If just ONE of these books can actually shift your thinking from scrambling week-to-week or month-to-month to confidently flowing from YEAR-to-YEAR, then you're well on your way to creating wealth and financial independence for you and your family for generations to come.

I kid you not – for generations to come.

It'd be my absolute honor to help you get there.

INTRODUCTION

You're awesome!

How's that for an introduction?

You are awesome because you already have everything you need inside to create financial independence one day for you and your family. The financial puzzle pieces are all there, you just need to solve it as you learn to Think Wealthy.

Personally, I could have avoided YEARS of student loan and credit card debt if only someone would have taught me how to think wealthy sooner.

You can LEARN to be wealthy or financially independent – or BOTH – because the rules by which you make money and your MONEY makes money are simple and only need to be learned once.

I'm living proof of that.

I went from being the poorest guy in any room to a self-made first-generation millionaire and I'm going to show you how I did it.

There are plenty of great financial planners out there and they are easy enough to hire (and you SHOULD hire one at some point), but what has protected me and my family and what will protect YOU, too, in the long run is for you to "get it" – for you to "get" money. Because once you get it, you got it…and you'll never forget it.

Tell me if this sounds familiar…

No one ever shared with you everything they knew about money – how money works in the world, what it's really for and, most importantly, how to make as much of it as you want in your lifetime – I never heard it from my parents, grandparents, teachers and I'm guessing you never heard it, either.

Sucks to be just the two of us, right?

Turns out it's a LOT more than just the two of us because nearly 80% of Americans live paycheck-to-paycheck which means they don't "get" money yet, either.

80% of Americans, or over 100 million people, live paycheck to paycheck in the wealthiest country the world has ever known – SAY WHAT?!?

If misery loves company then there's a big 'ol party going on in the U.S. of A.

Which is exactly why I am writing these books. So we can stop commiserating in our negative net worth and start celebrating our financial freedom TOGETHER.

My Goal of Zero Net Worth

For years my highest financial aspiration was to simply break even and have a net worth of zero.

I can't believe I'm sharing that. It's so ridiculous.

I LITERALLY used to dream about having no debt and no assets to my name. "What a financial god I'll be when I finally have ZERO dollars to my name instead of all this debt! I'm going to shout it from the rooftops and people will dance behind me as I'm asked to lead endless parades around town."

My life's highest financial goal for the longest time was to JUST BREAK EVEN in the financial game of life.

Silly, goofy money-unsavvy Todd. Now that we have our retirement years accounted for, the memory stings a little bit less, but it's still embarrassing to admit.

But you know what? How many people reading this right now might have the exact same financial goal that I did?

"Man, if I can just get to ZERO net worth, I'll be better off than everyone I know!"

All I had heard from my parents and teachers was to get good grades and work hard and that the financial stuff would take of itself.

That was a lie.

The financial stuff does NOT just take care of itself…at least not without understanding how money works in the world and how YOU can make it work hard for you in your own life.

From Poorest Guy in Any Room to 1st Generation Millionaire

I'll keep the details of my life to a relative minimum as we're here to talk about YOU, but suffice it to say that since college I have found relative success in many different areas of the fickle, über-competitive entertainment industry in Hollywood, sticking with a particular career only until it no longer paid emotional dividends.

In terms of education, I double-majored in Linguistics and French in undergrad and was a graduate student at the USC School of Cinema-Television. I worked in commercial casting, I was a successful commercial actor appearing in spots for Volkswagen, Subway, Sears, Westin Hotels, Men Are From Mars Women Are From Venus board game and on and on..., I was a reality TV casting manager traveling the country for MTV before transitioning to a Director of Marketing and Account Director role for a digital creative agency that worked with all the major movie studios and premium cable channels to help them market their shows and movies online through any digital channel and platform we could think of. Most recently, I have worked as the Head of Growth for an awesome boutique branding agency based in the L.A. area.

I was also a film projectionist for a work-study job in college (did you ever see *Cinema Paradiso*?) and then to some of the wealthiest and most famous of the Hollywood elite. I used to drive to people's homes in Beverly Hills, BelAir, Pacific Palisades, Malibu…homes worth tens and even hundreds of millions of dollars to project 35-millimeter prints of the latest films in their private screening rooms. (Before the digital revolution hit its tipping point and everyone started just pushing buttons at home.)

What's a few hundred dollars they would pay me for an in-home film screening of the newest releases when you're not paying that crazy upcharge on popcorn and soda at the theater, amirite?

I used to peek out from the port windows at the lavish screening rooms filled with popcorn machines and endless jars filled to the brim with candy and think, "What is so different between them and me? What do they know about money that I don't? And how do I get to THAT side of life?"

Financially-speaking, I've had windfalls of money roll in over the years from commercial residual checks, I've been unemployed and collecting funemployment for months at a time in-between reality casting gigs and I have humbly and frugally lived with a stable six-figure income, replete with 401k and quarterly sales bonuses.

Through all those careers and adventures I have seen both sides of the coin, having nothing to my name for decades when I was easily the poorest guy in any room, to seeing how "the other half" lived in their amazing mansions and now to making a beeline straight for a wealthy, happy and healthy life for myself and my family.

My partner and I have gone from a negative net worth of over $50,000 when we met fifteen years ago to being squarely on track to become 1st generation millionaires.

We have zero debt and our FICO scores are well into the 800s. Life ain't bad on the financial front…and it's only getting better.

And yet, none of this would have been possible if I didn't learn how to Think Wealthy. Swing a dead cat (as the saying goes) and you could easily hit another couple with all the same life circumstances but who are now even MORE in debt.

What's the difference between us and them?

Welcome to the Think Wealthy Series

I'm fascinated by what's called the psychology of wealth…the idea that simply how you THINK about money directly affects how much money you HAVE.

Yet it's absolutely true.

Regardless of how much I struggled to be better with my money than my parents were, for years (and years and years) I just barely got by.

Just like them.

Saddled with consumer debt I lived paycheck to paycheck just like my parents always did (and the 80% of the rest of Americans).

But who could blame my parents? If they knew better they would have shared it with me and my sister, too – they only want the best for us, right?

The U.S. is always touted as the wealthiest nation ever to exist in the modern era – but if we can't create and pass down our collective financial wisdom to successive generations, we don't deserve to hang onto that title for much longer.

What we're talking about in this book is having it ALL – more financial means than you need in one lifetime (if you want), an inner confidence against whatever life tries to throw your way (did I mention yet that I was diagnosed with cancer in March of 2021? #lifehappens), being surrounded by a supportive, loving family and a wealth of true friends who get you and who inspire you (and whom you inspire) to be ever better people in the world.

That's what I call WELL-ROUNDED WEALTH and it's what I want for you and your family – we'll talk more about this in the final book in the series.

I didn't realize it at the time, for those decades of early adulthood, but debt made me feel LESS THAN in life – it made me feel that I actually had less VALUE as a human being than other people…and that I certainly had less value than anyone with the appearance of financial success.

For years I mistakenly confused my NET WORTH with my SELF WORTH and as a wide-eyed man-child buried under $60,000 of consumer debt from student loans and credit cards who was entering the labor force, I made way too many mistakes that actually kept me from growing up financially (and emotionally) – it was a diaper of debt.

Are you, too, wearing a diaper of debt? (I may be the first Financial Poet Laureate!)

As you can imagine, now that I've figured it out for myself, I'm over-the-moon excited to talk about money with everyone else.

I love the peace of mind and the sense of safety, security and freedom that having money in the bank has afforded us. Heck, it created the space for me to not just TALK about this book (everyone has a book or ten in them), but actually sit down and WRITE it.

I wish I had read this book in high school before going to college and then again as I headed out into the world as a young pup (with the saddest excuse for a moustache the world has ever seen).

I also wish I had this book at my disposal when I needed to be reminded of how powerful I was in creating my OWN life and doing it with confidence and purpose.

The biggest gift you can give yourself, and my singular goal in writing these books, is for you to be confident with your money because it will mean you are also confident with the decisions in most every other area of your life.

Besides, I've done the bulk of the work in writing it down – all you have to do is READ the dern thing and think about yourself!

The Goal of This Think Wealthy Book Series

My singular goal in writing this book series is to change your entire relationship with money.

For the better.

Forever.

(I like to aim low.)

And we're going to have fun along the way because life just isn't as serious as we've made it out to be.

By the end of these books, if I've done my job, you will be excited about money, creating more of it, investing it, donating it...letting it flow through you to do good and make even MORE MONEY in the world.

And you'll do it all in good conscience so you can sleep soundly at night.

I envision a country whose citizens aren't on the collective brink of collapse, where its people AND its government don't spend above their means.

It sickens me that the majority of Americans do not have even a spare $1,000 in a bank account, that they don't know that they SHOULD have it tucked away and understand WHY – it should scare the bejeezus out of all of us.

Luckily for you and for anyone who dares to crack the digital pages of this book, there are only a few timeless facts about money and wealth you need to learn. If you don't have these basics at the very center of your financial worldview informing the money decisions you make day in and day out, you'll probably never make a lot of money…or at least you certainly won't KEEP much of it.

I'm proud of my Midwestern heritage – I just wish it didn't take me 40 years to figure out the basic financial concepts of wealth creation and wealth management!

Before we dig into what the wealthy already know about money, let's take any of the sting out of the word "wealth" first.

Do you want to be wealthy?

You scream, "YES!" in your mind, but then shrink back because you may not know anyone who IS wealthy and it feels greedy when you're surrounded by friends and family who are always struggling to get by. Or maybe it sounds too hoity-toity to be wealthy and you just want to keep it real, yo. Or whatever other of a thousand negative responses you may have associated with the word "wealth."

To me, wealth is simply having MORE money tomorrow than you have today. That's it.

Wealth is nothing more than having more money tomorrow than you have today.

Wealth is having a higher net worth tomorrow than you do today.

Not a million dollars more – but even five dollars more – each day – quickly adds up.

So do you want to be wealthy – do you want to have progressively more money day after day?

If you are tired of throwing your monthly bills across the room to hit the snooze button on the life you've always wanted, then let's grab a cup of joe or an awesome craft beer (it must be 5pm somewhere right now) and let's figure this out together.

The point of this fourth book in the Personal Finance series is to show you HOW to Think Wealthy because, if you don't have this in place, you will never BECOME wealthy.

Everyone who wants to think wealthy, please turn the page…now!

THINKING WEALTHY

Here are the facts, Jack and Jackie.

We are the product of our thoughts, for better or for worse, and most definitely for richer or for poorer.

Literally, as the cement dries at the foundation of your belief system from the last book, _Meet Your Inner Billionaire_, your future as a wealthy individual all boils down to HOW YOU THINK.

Just as how you currently think was learned, how you start to think moving forward can be drilled into your noodle just as easily, until it becomes second nature.

If you learned to think working or middle-class (as most of us did growing up), you can also learn to Think Wealthy.

I want to say this again because it's that important:

When you THINK wealthy, you BECOME wealthy.

Wealth can be learned.

I learned it and it turned my life around. For years I couldn't catch my breath because I had so much student loan and credit card debt. Now that we have been debt-free for ten years, it's almost hard to remember that crushing feeling – but I do know I will never go back.

To think wealthy is to pull yourself into financial freedom, whether that means maintaining and protecting your wealth for generations to come or spending what you need and giving the rest away at the end of your days.

The larger point is that our minds are infinitely powerful – it's up to us whether we direct them toward the strongest or weakest results in our lives.

I think I know what choice you've made if you're reading this book.

Let's dive right in...

THE THOUGHT POLICE – FROM FOE TO FLOW

It's no great revelation to say that thoughts bubble up in our consciousness constantly, day in and day out. We are all certifiably insane, crazy, cuckoo-headed human beings when it comes to the self-chatter bouncing around between our ears.

If we were able to step back and objectively look at the constant deluge of thoughts jockeying for attention inside our heads, we'd run straight for the state loony bin – the nut house, the funny farm, the booby hatch.

("Todd, that's not very mature or woke of you to call it those names. The people who live there have mental illnesses and deserve our respect and sympathy." See?

There was another thought...one *reprimanding* me for an earlier thought – UGH!)

Our minds are so cluttered it's amazing that we get *anything* done, isn't it? All those images (it's called 'image-ination,' after all) and words in the form of affirmations, judgments, opinions, short-term repetitions, superstitions – our minds are a chaotic symphony that has lost its place on the sheet music and refuses to obey the conductor.

But the conductor is YOU!

Sure, you can meditate and learn to bring yourself a moment or two of silence, but the unending barrage of thoughts is a fact of life for all of us. I don't care if you're the Dalai Lama (and if you are, congrats on living on such a low clothing budget), your mind is still going to be an untamed stallion running free across the plains.

But we need it! If we didn't have thought, we wouldn't be as civilized a people as we are. Thought is the very cornerstone of our humanity so I don't have anything against thinking…or thoughts, per se.

What concerns me about thoughts is that most people don't realize how POWERFUL their thoughts are or that they spend most of their time distracted by the shiny-object-ness of inconsequential thoughts, not to mention a constant negative self-talk that so many of us have simply acclimated to over the years.

Most of us have fallen under the spell of our rambling brain chitchat and take it all at face value – we blindly trust the veracity of the chatter in our head without ever asking for proof.

** HEY – Are you still with me or are you LOST IN YOUR THOUGHTS AGAIN? **

By learning to Think Wealthy we can at least get the money section of the symphony playing in tune and harmonizing.

Yep, I'm saying that by training your thoughts on money, by monitoring and policing them to keep them on the up and up, the positive effects will rub off on other areas of your life. In fact, they HAVE to.

Our Thoughts Pack a Real Punch

The reality is that most of us spend way too much of our mental energy beating ourselves up or placing imaginary obstacles in our own way. It's total bedlam in your head sometimes, isn't it? It is in *mine*!

Which is okay.

For now.

It's just your ego parroting someone else in your life (probably a parent or other family member) because that's all it knows. It thinks it's protecting you, but once it learns how to *actually* support you, your life can change practically overnight.

Check out this common phrase I overheard my parents say to themselves while I was growing up:

"You dummy, why did you put the plate back in the dishwasher when it was already clean…[or insert random activity here]?"

They wouldn't talk to me or my sister that way. They talked to themSELVES that way. It was their self-talk.

But it wasn't just one parent. No, my sister and I were the lucky recipients of BOTH of our parents berating themselves when they did any silly thing where they "just should have known better."

So, guess what amusing and destructive self-talk I took out into the world AND guess how many decades it took me to stop thinking that I was an idiot or dumb for not realizing that that plate was already clean when I put it back in the dishwasher, too?

Our thoughts are indicators of our deeper, subconscious beliefs – that thought pattern I inherited from my parents was the tipoff to a belief I had that I was barely smart enough to navigate my own kitchen and that surely *everyone else* in the world had more common sense than I did.

But wait – this story has a happy ending!

Now I don't call myself an idiot any longer – consciously or unconsciously – I have broken the cycle and it has become my life's mission to make sure our daughter doesn't hear it or internalize it, either – not from us, at least.

It's also my life's mission to ensure that YOU don't do it, either – whether we're talking about a clean plate or your ability to create wealth for you and your family.

Breaking the Cycle of Negative Self-Talk

I now forgive myself for any silly mistakes I make because they simply don't matter against the backdrop of my long-term goals – I also know it's a poor use of the limited time any of us have left on this spinning rock of minerals to replay these inconsequential mental moments ad nauseum.

What helped me past that roadblock was learning to change my thinking and to treat myself with the respect I deserve.

Thinking Wealthy is an expanded and positive way of thinking that will sound alarm bells for you every time you catch yourself thinking this way or hearing someone else verbalize a negative and defeating thought.

When I met my partner, we were both guided by a predominant middle-class mentality of "just surviving" month-to-month because we were saddled with so much consumer debt. By talking about money and setting common goals together, however – by challenging our way of thinking about money – we turned around our financial lives. And best of all we did it together.

We even turned it into a game – a healthy competition – to see who could get out credit card debt first!

We can all train ourselves to think a certain way, in a way that empowers us in any facet of our lives (financial matters, weight loss, self-esteem, happiness) – we can do this by putting the cart before the horse (or perhaps the cart before the untamed stallion running wild across the plains) because with the repetition of powerful thoughts, ever-stronger beliefs form deep within as we saw in the last book, *Meet Your Inner Billionaire*.

This is the part of the book where I say that if I can do it, you can do it, too. I don't know if you believe that yet, but I stand behind it 100%.

Besides, what better use do you have for your time while you're on the bus or stuck in traffic or standing in line at the bank (do people still go into banks?) or grocery store or Starbucks – use that time for some mental gymnastics just north of your eyeballs.

Financial Cruising Altitude

Before we dig into your brain like a zombie (#nomnom), let me give you a little context for the 10 ways of thinking wealthy that I've created here.

Think of these ten thoughts as your 30,000-foot view of your life and your finances. When you're cruising that high in the sky and looking down on everything, it's easiest to see the big picture. You won't hear all the noise at ground level – all that mental chatter we've been talking about. We're more analytical at cruising altitude, and less emotional.

If you're ever feeling stuck or unmotivated in your life, look back over these ten points and get back into the air at a higher altitude to see if you've strayed from any of these ways of thinking and acting.

Right before we take flight into our brain and poke around at our thoughts together, let's take another look at The Money Dam™ as I'll be referencing it throughout this book.

THE MONEY DAM

I created the money dam because I find it to be a very powerful metaphor for thinking about your own money – it'll be our visual metaphor as we dive deeper into our money talk together.

Much as the same water is always recirculating throughout the world and you statistically drink some of the very water molecules that made their way through Julius Caesar ("Et tu, reader?")… or through a dinosaur (RAWR!)…money is always in a similar flow around the globe.

Think of the accumulation of your money as water being saved up behind a dam, thus creating a lake. Just like water in a real reservoir, any money you have in the bank is in reserve.

[This is a simplified version of The Money Dam. For the free full-color final version, go to: thinkwealthybook.com]

Your money, your net worth, is like water behind a dam. Just as dams let water through to generate electricity or to fulfill contracts to provide water downstream, you do this, too, when you pay for... anything! The biggest dams don't completely block the flow of water, but they do limit its flow downstream from what they receive upstream just as you can limit the outflow of your own money based on your financial choices.

Water behind a dam is stored up as potential energy.

A few people have a Hoover Dam/Lake Mead of resources at their disposal (Bill Gates, Mark Zuckerberg, Warren Buffett, Bernard Arnault...any billionaire, for sure) and many people have a reservoir that could last perhaps a decade of income drought of retirement, but most Americans who live paycheck-to-paycheck have at best a few twigs of good intentions bunched together that don't stop any of the water from flowing right past them downstream.

People with a NEGATIVE net worth and little to no income, which was my situation for years and years when I was saddled with student loan debt, feel like there's only desert as far as the eye can see. For this latter group, there is no dam to build because there has never been any water to hold back.

For our Lake of Net Worth to rise, we first need to build our dam even higher and for that we only need to learn to Think Wealthy.

As I always say, "If you don't give a dam about your money, no one else will!"

THINK WEALTHY #1: THINK NET WORTH, NOT SALARY

This is a great one to start with because we constantly hear which jobs pay the highest salary as if that's the only thing that matters when it comes to our money.

For decades, everyone was told to become a doctor or a lawyer if they wanted to make the big bucks. Then engineering hit the radar screen and, of course, Wall Street bankers and hedge fund managers were added to the mix. And now we're all supposed to be coders and tech entrepreneurs starting private companies that turn into unicorns when they go public, the new American dream.

We are still told that the good jobs are the ones that pay the best. And to get them, we have to study hard and go to the right schools.

Sure, we may graduate with over $100,000 in student loan debt that will ultimately cost us $145,000 after we factor in the compounding interest, but that's the price for a good education so you can make a decent income, right?

Because financial freedom is all about our salary, right? RIGHT?

WRONG!

Back in the day I read that the wealthy measure their money in terms of their NET WORTH and not how much INCOME they bring in in a year.

(Here comes the embarrassing part...)

I actually thought, "Net worth?!? What does THAT have to do with anything?" (As the guy who dreamed of having a zero net worth for years because of his debt, you can see why I might have been a tad confused.)

Now I know, of course, that net worth is the ONLY benchmark the wealthy (and those who write about them) use.

But how ingrained was it in my Midwestern psyche that the only barometer of wealth was a person's SALARY at their JOB?

[If you don't know how to calculate your net worth, you simply take the value of everything you OWN (or all your assets: real estate, cars, bank accounts, retirement accounts) and subtract everything you OWE (or all your debts: mortgages, car loans, credit card balances, student loans).

That beautiful remaining number is your net worth.]

Looking at The Money Dam, your net worth is the water, or lake of assets, rising up behind the dam as it rises throughout your life.

For decades I had a negative net worth because in assets I had an average of $2,000 in a checking account and a Honda Civic (of ever decreasing value as that's what cars do best, they *lose* value or depreciate) that was worth $7,500. So, my assets were $9,500, but the debt of my student loans was $60,000. Take the $9,500 of assets and subtract $60,000 of liabilities and I had a net worth of negative $50,500 (-$50,500).

Negative net worth. For decades. Good times!

It felt crushing. As I've said elsewhere, I felt like I could never catch my breath. No wonder I didn't know the value of tracking my net worth – who would?!?

Before I earned a six-figure salary myself, I erroneously thought the more money a person MADE, the more money they… just…HAD because there was that much more "excess" money in their paycheck.

I soon learned, however, that between higher tax brackets and living a larger, more expansive and expensive lifestyle, most people who make more money don't FEEL any excess coming in from month to month because they've slowly scaled up their living as they've earned more money. In fact, for many people, it's just as easy to live paycheck to paycheck on multiple six figures as it is on the $46,000 lower end of middle class.

What someone makes as INCOME has very little to do with their NET WORTH. As the saying goes…

It's not what you earn, it's what you keep.

It is true, however, that the more money you make, the more likely you are to be increasing your net worth by maxing out your retirement accounts and making other healthy financial decisions. If you're making $200,000 a year, for example, there is a baseline financial education that often comes along with that type of salary – it won't be your first job so you'll already know about 401(k)s and the other financial options available to you as an employee. If nothing else, you're working with people at the same income level and them sharing their financial best practices will educate you, too.

This may be news to you, but collecting a SALARY at a JOB makes it near impossible to become wealthy because you lose so much off the top to income taxes.

Add in lifestyle creep that comes with an increase in salary and the nice Instagrammable picture on the outside shows nothing of the financial health on the inside.

How often do you hear of the family that drives a new Mercedes their whole life but have little in retirement – yet a custodian at the local public high school leaves 10 million to his favorite charity when he or she died?

These flipped-script financial stories tend to make the rounds during recessions when the kimono opens on people's otherwise private financial lives.

Ultimately, no one knows what goes on behind closed doors. Your blandly-dressed neighbor may be a millionaire next door while friends who live in the biggest houses lose sleep each night worrying about their finances.

Net worth, everyone's lake of net worth, makes the difference. It is the only metric that can be reliably used to determine an individual or family's financial health and strength.

Forbes magazine ranks the richest Americans and billionaires by their net worth, naturally – if they listed the wealthiest people by salary, the "brand name" billionaire CEOs we all know wouldn't even make the list as so many of them take $1 salary per year. Besides being a savvy political move so shareholders will believe the CEO is more concerned about raising overall stock value than draining cash from the company with a big salary, every CEO knows that taxes paid on income, or salary, will be higher than on other forms of executive compensation like stock options.

One of the best advantages for thinking net worth over salary is that it conditions us to think of money as an asset (something that grows in value) rather than thinking of money as income (something that you spend).

The ENTIRE PURPOSE of this book series, in fact, is for you to start thinking of every dollar to your name as an ASSET that can grow in value instead of thinking of your money as income to be spent.

◆ ◆ ◆

Wealth Tip: Think in terms of appreciating assets.

As our net worth should always be increasing, the primary way to do that is by investing only in *appreciating assets*.

Yes, a new $45,000 car smells amazeballz, but it should hurt like a punch in the paunch for you to drive it off the lot since it will only lose value over its lifetime, not to mention the additional costs in maintenance and insurance on a higher-priced vehicle.

Of course, we all need to figure out the transportation piece of our lives, but even buying a two-year-old car with a dealership warranty at a fair market price makes stronger financial sense than buying a new car outright.

Wealthy people try not to spend money on things that decrease in value over time – it's that simple. If that sounds topsy-turvy, then you're still confusing wealth with materialism.

When you think of money as an ASSET, you only invest in things that will appreciate and turn into more money later on.

Appreciating assets over the long term tend to be stocks, real estate, currencies, fine art and other collectibles. Even in retirement, a truly wealthy mindset resists the idea of "spending down" the principal of the money they've saved and invested…the real goal is to live off the *interest* of your principal, so your lake of net worth never dips to a lower level.

I've never thought of myself as much of a negotiator, but I bought a smoked glass table that seated 6 for $200 when I moved into my first apartment. I used it for 10 years and after enough friends publicly shamed me into getting rid of it ("smoked glass, dude?!?"), I used a Sharpie to hide all the dings in the cheap metal frame and sold it for $200 on Craigslist.

Not bad, right? Sure, the $200 I spent for it was worth more than the $200 I received for it ten years later given the effects of inflation, but it was one of my first attempts to see what the market would bear. Win-win! Now someone else can be both proud of and shamed by their choice in dining room furniture.

We also bought a new, unused dishwasher from a friend for $100. We used it for 5 years and, before moving into a house that already had one, we sold the 5-year-old dishwasher for $160!

Why did I sell it for more than what I paid for it? Because $160 is what the market (or a couple with a baby about to drop) would pay for a good used dishwasher from someone who took good care of it.

I do not kid myself that these money moves will make us wealthy one day, but the mental machinations behind these sales are already in place and will work on a larger scale, too.

Years ago, I probably would've just given these items away as if they were worth nothing because I paid so little for them… but now I think of my money as an asset.

Whoever says furniture and appliances always depreciate hasn't been drawn into the tractor beam of my Craigslist marketing prowess!

◆ ◆ ◆

Wealth Tip: *Realize your network is your net worth.*

It is said (and there's even a book about it so it must be true!) that your network is your net worth. That means the five people you hang out with the most…their average net worth is going to be about on par with your net worth.

Stop right now and think of the five people you hang out with the most…who you're most real with…ask yourself if you're comfortable in the same net worth zone as them or do you have higher financial aspirations?

Do your closest friends always complain about not having enough money, not knowing where they're going to find the money for x, y, z or never talking about long-term goals and plans?

This makes sense on several levels since we tend to socialize with and even marry people of the same socioeconomic background in which we were raised, but the takeaway is that if you're not connected with people who will push your game even higher, if you're not meeting people who you can emulate and learn financial wisdom from, your financial future is laid out right in front of you.

The financial writing is on the wall.

◆ ◆ ◆

Wealth Warning: *Think of consumer debt as an STI to your financial health.*

Consumer debt (credit cards, auto loans, personal loans, even student loans if you don't have a plan or a bankable skillset to show for it) is like a sexually transmitted infection (STI) – it felt good when you got the debt because you weren't really thinking with the smartest parts of your body, but now you feel you may never shake that bug.

And unless you have a plan to get rid of it, it may hang on as long as you do!

For me, I heard Suze Orman's sharp Chicago twang screaming in my ear for years whenever I thought about purchasing something.

For years!

I watched her show every week – with a negative net worth and no retirement investments to my name, I would always hear her yelling at me to

DEEEEEENYYYY myself major purchases so that I could make it to a future day of financial freedom, which fortunately arrived much sooner than I thought it would.

Thanks, Suze, for helping me change my world from the inside out! I'll give you a big hug one day, GIRLFRIEND.

The truth is that most people seem to be comfortable with a certain level of consumer debt. They dig themselves out of the hole a little bit and then buy more shtuff because the monthly payments (which are loaded with interest, of course) already fit well into their monthly spending – besides, what the heck is excess money for if not for buying more things you think you need, right?

If it helps, think of revolving debt (anything with monthly installment payments – credit cards, auto loans, student loans) as you setting your hard-earned money on fire and watching it go up in smoke. Gone. Not so much for the thing you bought with that money, but for all the interest being charged month after month until it's paid off.

To be clear, you don't OWN anything that you buy with a credit card until it's fully paid off. It is not "yours" until that balance is zero.

Consumer debt anchors you to the past making it nearly impossible to see a brighter future.

◆ ◆ ◆

Money Math*: Daily cost of revolving debt.*

If you want to motivate yourself out of revolving debt, figure out how much you're paying in interest EVERY SINGLE DAY on your debt.

I did this with my student loans at one point and it took me to new depths of financial despair to see that I owed $5 a day just in interest on those loans. I realized that if I wasn't earning at least $5 each day (including weekends), then I wasn't even breaking even on what I owed and my debt would just continue to snowball UP from there.

Looking at the larger population, if the average American household carries credit card debt of $5,525 at a 16% interest rate, that means their debt is costing them $2.42 a day, or $72.61 a month. And that's not paying down any of the principal, that's just to break even.

If you have a similar debt load, think of the first $2.42 you make each day as just going out to pay for the honor of using the credit card company's money.

When you wake up each morning knowing how much you need to earn JUST to break even with any capitalizing interest you owe, it can either send you back under the covers to sing the blues or motivate you into action – both of which I've experienced over the years.

◆ ◆ ◆

Wealth Warning: *Debt résumé.*

As I like to say, if you carry a student loan or credit card balance forward each month, you're really working for the banks because some of the money you earn really belongs to them.

I worked for Capital One and MBNA for YEARS until I made a lateral move and was transferred (via a balance transfer – oh yes, I did!) to work for Discover Card for another few years.

So, who do YOU work for…Amex…Bank of America…Chase? Whoever you owe money to owns a small piece of your soul at the cost of your sense of safety, security and freedom in the world.

Back to The Money Dam analogy, there is a hole at the base of your dam that belongs to whoever you owe money to and the only way to shore up that leak is to pay it off as soon as you can.

THINK WEALTHY #2: THINK LONG-TERM

This is the most crucial piece to thinking wealthy, period.

I feared I may never learn this because I had whiled away most of my life only living and thinking short-term or month-to-month.

Sure, I may have set long-term goals in terms of career, but they were more like dreams floating in between my ears *without any real plan of action*.

It's said that the middle class thinks month-to-month.

And who could blame them when we all live in a monthly bill cycle? It's perfectly natural to use a month as a financial benchmark because that's what we've all been CONDITIONED to do – get a job that meets our monthly needs and then increase our lifestyle (bigger house, newer car, more lavish vacations) with each promotion or pay raise we receive.

By thinking month-to-month, the middle class creates a lifestyle where whatever money comes in, goes right back out. Pretty logical thinking, actually – it's just too nearsighted for creating actual wealth.

If the middle class thinks month-to-month, then the working class (or working poor as they're sometimes called) think week-to-week. They're in survival mode, pure and simple.

Often the working class is not even living week-to-week - they may have been forced into payday loans because it's their only option. With those atrocious interest rates, you could say the working class are stuck in the past, scraping by just to catch up to month-to-month middle-class thinking which is often only one sneeze away from financial ruin, anyway!

How can you move forward with your life when you still haven't paid for the things you bought last week, last month or last year?

If the working poor are bound to the past and the middle class are just keeping their heads above water month-to-month, it stands to reason that the wealthy or upper class are thinking more long-term – in fact, the wealthy think year-to-year. Decade-to-decade even!

To think long-term is to Think Wealthy.

This is why they take smart risks – they have the financial stability today to bet on a bigger payoff or payout down the line.

This is what you see on ABC's hit show *Shark Tank* – a GREAT primer on entrepreneurship if ever there were one. The sharks don't need the investments they make to pay off immediately to keep food on the table, they have a long-term view and can afford to wait years to recoup a healthy return on their investments, all the while creating jobs and contributing cool new products and services to the economy.

If you want to be wealthy, you must think long-term.

◆ ◆ ◆

Wealth Tip: *Think of every dollar you earn as a seed of your financial future.*

Then water those financial seeds.

Every dollar you make has the potential to make many more dollars for the future.

This is what motivates the wealthy – they know that every dollar they make today may be worth ten more next year or a thousand more in ten years. They're thinking long-term.

If you remember the difference between cash and money from the first book in this series, *Understand Money*, think of CASH coming in and going right back out, but MONEY grows over time.

Earn more than you spend and invest the rest – dam up your money to raise your lake of net worth!

Keep top of mind that putting $50,000 into a retirement account by the age of 25, earning 8% a year will turn into $1,000,000 by the age of 65.

It's not hard to be a millionaire if that's your highest financial aspiration...

◆ ◆ ◆

Wealth Tip: *Figure out cash flow for life.*

Since your only job (and mine...and everyone you know's job) is to figure out how to pay your monthly bills until game over – if you can make a plan for cash flow for life and DO it, a very real version of wealth can be yours.

This is a somewhat modern version of wealth – it's not dependent on amassing a lakeful of net worth (and assets) that will create wealth for generations to come – it is figuring how what your specific monthly needs are now and for years to come and saving and investing up to a pre-determined amount that you will then spend down or seeking out specific passive income assets that will cover those needs month after month after month. Or some combination of the two.

We'll cover both types of wealth creation in the next book in the series, *Create Your Fortune, Big or Small*.

This monthly cash flow strategy is the basis behind the FIRE (Financial Independence, Retire Early) Movement which is gaining popularity as Millennials and Gen Zers reach for the rip cord from the rat race.

FIRE is based on choosing your own day of "retirement." In its most basic form, you determine your FIRE number by multiplying your annual expenses by 25 and then you live a substantially frugal lifestyle while saving and investing up to 75% of your take-home income until you hit that number which you then spend down at a rate of 4% each year.

A FIRE strategy can take the form of traditional tax-advantaged retirement accounts, taxable brokerage accounts for funds needed before reaching 59.5 years of age and income-producing investment properties like single or multi-family homes.

Cash flow wealth differs from the traditional meaning of wealth in that you won't get a building named after you at your alma mater, but you'll be wealthy in the sense of never running out of money for your monthly bills.

Robert Kiyosaki was the first author and investor I can think of who brought the primacy of cash flow to the fore with his bestselling book *Rich Dad, Poor Dad*. He even created the *CASHFLOW Board Game* in case you weren't sure where he stood on the issue of wealth creation.

I had read Kiyosaki's bestselling book, but it didn't resonate with me until Paul Sullivan, wealth columnist for the New York Times and author of the *The Thin Green Line: The Money Secrets of the Super Wealthy*, wrote that you don't need a lot of money in the bank to be considered wealthy – what you need is a solid cash flow plan for the rest of your life.

Just as it may look like I'm repeating myself from time to time within the pages of this book series – I promise you it's intentional – it took me reading about the cash flow strategy a few times before it truly sunk in.

Figuring out monthly cash flow is very PROACTIVE and IMMEDIATE – you are working to get to financial freedom ASAP as opposed to waiting for an official retirement age (in your 60s) when Social Security kicks in and you can start drawing down tax-advantaged retirement accounts.

It is based on you determining an exact number that you can comfortably live on whereas traditional wealth creation in the Sara Blakely or Elon Musk model has no real ceiling to their net worth – they're not trying to afford a certain lifestyle – the businesses they created that underpin their wealth have unlimited upside potential.

If you can strategize your own cash flow for life and start implementing that plan today, you'll be in full financial control one day in the future. I'd tell you to go ahead and skip to the end of this book series if that's what you're doing, but then you'd miss all my remaining Dad jokes...and my ego strongly advises you against that.

◆ ◆ ◆

Wealth Tip: Bucket!

This is a mental trick that wealthy people do naturally and you will, too, once you start beefing up your net worth.

One of the easiest ways to get your synapses to start thinking and planning long-term is to think of your money as being divvied up into separate buckets. If you currently lump all your money together in your mind, start with three buckets, one each for safety, security and freedom.

These three buckets start filling up *after* you've met your monthly bills for rent/mortgage, food, utilities, transportation, insurance(s), other monthly needs, shopping and entertainment.

Here are the three primary buckets:

1) **Safety** (Saving): The first bucket is a savings account which you maintain to keep you feeling SAFE in the short-term.

   If your laptop is about to die or your tooth aches after a bag of Skittles and it's only getting worse…this account is for money that you will need in the relative short-term (within FIVE YEARS).

   This bucket sits in a different account than one for monthly living because it's doing something completely different – it's protecting you – you're not living in fear of life's little surprises – it makes you feel safe. If money for monthly living sits in a checking account, the Safety bucket sits in a savings account.

You can think of this as your emergency fund if you want, the goal being that you're never dependent on using a credit card to get you out of a pinch. Only use credit cards if you can pay them off in full at the end of each month while gladly accepting their cashback rewards.

Each month this safety account goes up and up and up with the occasional down for a replacement laptop or crown on your back tooth…then up, up, up, down a little, up, up, up, down a little, up, up, up, up…

2) **Security** (Investing): The second bucket is an investment account (or several of them!) to keep you secure for the future, for the long term.

These are tax-advantaged retirement accounts or taxable investment accounts where you automate money into it from each check and LEAVE IT THERE so that it can grow and grow and grow.

These accounts may be a 401(k) if the company you work for offers one or your own investment accounts easily set up at a TD Ameritrade or Charles Schwab or another online broker. These aren't necessarily accounts for gambling with the latest new crypto craze or whatever is coming around the corner next – these accounts are there to create long-term Security for your future. It's your life and you can invest however you like, but most people ride the market (mostly) up in diversified mutual funds or ETFs.

These accounts may bounce up and down in the short term based on the stock and bond markets or whatever you're invested in, but your long-term perspective in this bucket only goes up and up and up…

3) **Freedom** (Your Plan + Your Execution): This third bucket is not as much an account as it is your *unique* vision for your own future financial freedom.

While the first two buckets work together like gears of a driveshaft to keep your life running smoothly, the freedom bucket is YOUR particular plan for financial independence if you decide to create one.

Your plan may very well involve your current skillsets but with a future payout date if you own your own business…or perhaps it's a separate venture you will invest in, one that provides massive value to others, and for which the market will willingly compensate you in return.

Your freedom plan is as unique as you are.

It's been shown time and time again that the wealthy bucket their finances – they mentally separate their money into different buckets to fulfill the different short and **long-term** goals they have – "bucketing" your finances is one of the easiest and most effective ways to take control of your financial life.

Other ways to bucket to get your mental juices flowing:

Create a **Vacation Account** where you save up for a big trip or create an ongoing **Investment/Education Account** where you set aside $50 or $100 a month for your continuing education on your way to financial freedom.

When you plan out your buckets, there is no confusion with what your money is supposed to do when it flows in each month because you've said upfront that this is where you want it to go and what you want it to do.

◆ ◆ ◆

Wealth Tip: Plan for the worst, expect the best.

This is the sign that you're a financial adult in the world. You plan for the worst possible scenario (which is why you carry life, disability and other insurances to mitigate your risks and protect your loved ones and your money - more on that in the final book in the series), but you expect the best.

How many more stories must we hear about the bread-winning father unexpectedly dying without any life insurance in place or the young parents not surviving a car accident with no living will or trust in place on how to divvy up their assets and protect their newborn child?

With life being the unpredictable fate cauldron that it is, this mantra of planning for the worst but expecting the best will also serve you well in every aspect of life, not just finances.

If something unexpected happens, what's your Plan B? Learn to think in terms of Plans A, B and C – by planning ahead, you are able to act fast when you need to because you've already done your homework and can course-correct with confidence.

My Broadway singer friend and I watched the YouTube video of Idina Menzel missing her top note in the live finale of the Frozen song "Let It Go" one chilly evening. She held onto that missed note for dear life as blood ran out of our ears. My friend yelled at the screen, "Idina, girl! How could you not have a Plan B?"

It was cold out (Times Square on New Year's Eve) and her voice was exhausted from doing 8 shows a week of another Broadway show – but she is a professional singer, an expert at her craft – how could she not have a Plan B for that final note?

One would expect that years of training and experience on stage should have instilled in Idina to plan for the worst but expect the best. That missed note probably has its own Twitter account.

◆ ◆ ◆

Wealth Tip: *This is your money! But it's only money!*

Total Contradiction Alert, I realize.

Hear me out.

THIS IS YOUR MONEY. NO ONE WILL TAKE BETTER CARE OF IT THAN YOU.

NO ONE WILL GIVE A BIGGER DAM ABOUT YOUR MONEY THAN YOU WILL.

BUT IT'S ONLY MONEY. DON'T TAKE IT ALL SO SERIOUSLY.

YET STILL TAKE IT DEADLY SERIOUSLY – DAM IT!

When you treat yourself with the respect you deserve, you will quickly know WHAT you want to spend money on and WHY. And you will be able to communicate that clearly to whomever you wish. You said yes to that destination wedding because you said yes. You said no to that destination winter ski trip because you said no. End of story.

At the same time, we're *only* talking about money here. People take it way too seriously as if they'll JUST DIE if they run out of it at any moment. As we've seen, though, money isn't anything more than a tool that provides us with safety or security or freedom or whatever it is that having money in the bank makes us feel.

And money is ABUNDANT so if you were to lose it all, you just go get more of the digital stuff already.

Realize that no one will take better care of your money than you will – but don't put money on a pedestal as it's really only good at doing a few things well.

I used this quote by P.T. Barnum at the very beginning of the first book in the series, _Understand Money_, that says…

Money is a terrible master but an excellent servant.

Be the master of your money – but create such a big life for yourself that it's nothing more than a piece of the puzzle, not the entire puzzle itself.

◆ ◆ ◆

_Wealth Warning__: Hope is not a financial plan._

If I had a dime for every time my mom confided in me that my parents were dancing on the cusp of financial ruin and not being able to pay their bills, but she cheerfully concluded that "everything always works out in the end," I'd be sipping Mai Thais with Richard Branson on the island I bought next to his.

Hope is not a financial plan.

(And I love you, Mom!)

Unfortunately, for millions of Americans, hope and prayers are the only financial plan many people have in place. They say it's because it's the easiest financial plan to make (which is true), but I think it's more because no one ever talked openly about money and showed them how to think wealthy for themselves.

If you get on a train, you expect the engineer driving the dern thing to know where he or she is going. Likewise, if you get in your car, you presumably have a destination in mind, you don't just hope you'll get where you want to go.

Why is money any different?

The truth is if you expect things to just barely work out, they will ALWAYS just barely work out. As they did for my parents. For decades.

If you want to really live your own life, though, you'll tell your money what you want IT to do and then the world can be your oyster.

◆ ◆ ◆

Wealth Warning: *The lottery is not a financial plan.*

Don't get me started.

Hopeful lottery winners think they will just win all that money and every problem will be solved.

Of course, they will be able to get out of debt and buy some shiny things, but if they've never had to manage large amounts of money before, any windfall will slip through their fingers as everyone they know shows up with their hands out for a piece of the pie – the money zombies show up with outstretched hands – and the newly rich will fritter it away, not knowing what else to do with it except SPEND it, losing all their friends in the process and wishing they'd never won the money in the first place.

If you haven't heard that a lottery is a tax on the poor, it is. You have much better odds of starting a successful business that actually fills a need in the marketplace.

I don't hate the lottery. I have "played" it with friends. To hope for immediate riches and to believe it might happen is a fun diversion for a few minutes, but only if you don't take it too seriously. Or DEPEND on it as an ACTUAL source of revenue.

Would I take the winnings? You betcha!

But I'd also take AMAZING care of that money, too.

THINK WEALTHY #3: THINK VALUE FIRST

Welcome to the funnest, never-ending game that you already play!

You may not realize you already think in terms of value, but you do. You do it everyday when you determine whether the organic bananas are worth the higher price or if the extra wax treatment at the car wash is worth the next tier of pricing – at every corner you look at the price of a good or service and determine whether the underlying value exists for you to buy it.

You may not think of this as a game, but it's a biggie. And it's a fun one!

To think wealthy, you always should be thinking about value within a larger context.

What do I mean by this…

If a larger flat-screen TV goes on sale and is a phenomenal deal, a real steal, even while your current one works just fine, that might look like a great value. In the context of not having any money behind your money dam, either in savings or a retirement account, though, the VALUE of that TV at *any price* should plummet.

There is little value in putting your future at risk for the sake of another object, another thing, that is not doing anything to help you make more money. A TV is not an investment – it's a depreciating asset just like a car – it provides no long-term return on your money.

Besides, you already have a TV that works just fine, remember?

The wealthy are always thinking of underlying value within that LONG-TERM time horizon we've already talked about.

Let's say you have a 5-year-old car that you just paid off that runs great – what's the value of buying a new car when you don't yet have enough money for health insurance?

Low. An unexpected illness without any insurance in place could saddle you with a hundred thousand dollars of debt practically overnight.

So far this year (2021), I've had close to two million dollars of unexpected health care expenses. If we didn't have health insurance in place, how much of that would I be on the hook for?!? We're still tabulating our out-of-pocket expenses as bills continue rolling in NINE MONTHS after the date of service, but it looks like we're only on the hook for less than .5% of the full $1,000,000 – phew!

What's the value of interning or volunteering for free for a few months to check out a possible new career field versus spending all your time at your current job dreaming only about the weekend ahead because you hate it so much?

High. Your passions may be shifting and you will make many valuable connections through volunteering to jumpstart a new career. On the flip side, you may discover that you really don't like performing experiments on chinchillas like you thought you would – but at least now you know!

I took an introductory personal finance course through UCLA Extension years ago because I was fascinated by talking about money. I didn't even make it halfway through the class before I bailed because it was…sooooooo…bloooody…borrrring. I wanted to scream, "This is MONEY we're talking about! Why have you drained it of any excitement? No really – of ANY excitement?"

Turns out I am more fascinated by the *psychology* of wealth than the nuts and bolts of personal finance. There are plenty of great financial planners out there who have taken that course and found their calling – what is lacking are people like me who want you to "get it," who want you to "get" money because once you get it, you got it, and you'll never forget or not get it.

That UCLA course cost me a few hundred dollars, but the lesson I learned made it worth it – HIGH value, for sure.

Learn to think of everything first in terms of value within a larger timeframe and context.

You can even do this with your current job.

What value do YOU bring to your employer? Rather than ask what value *they* bring to *you*, flip it and you'll see where you can improve in your own performance which will only reap more benefits for you.

Grant Cardone recently wrote something that completely shifted my view on "making money," which I was always told I had to do by my parents, my family, my teachers. They all told me, "You gotta *make* money, Todd!"

Grant says that it's a chore if you think of having to "make money." Instead, see yourself as COLLECTING MONEY because of the value you provide.

"Yes!" I thought to myself. This single shift could do amazing things for this country, not just in terms of work output, but in terms of helping people tap into their own happiness.

This may get a little dark, but what the heck – you can even play the value game in thinking about your friends. What VALUE do they bring to you? Do they lift you up and push you to dream even bigger, to achieve even more out of your life? And do YOU do the same for them? Or do you all just commiserate about how crappy everything is?

Some friends may be great brainstormers – they are great at helping you solve a problem or create something new you want for your life. Others may be friends who seem to know everyone – they can help you meet the right people to get to the next step toward a goal.

Learn to think of everything, even other people in terms of value – not in a creepy "What can you do for me?" way, but in the sense of achieving goals together. People really do want to help each other out.

By looking at everything through the lens of value, you'll naturally start to seek the things and experiences that bring you the most value in your life, which is completely unique to you.

Case in point...

A friend of mine bought a pen for a thousand dollars.

Then she lost it and decided to buy another one because she felt it was test from the universe and that she needed to proclaim (or reproclaim) her true worth.

I, on the other hand, will never pay more than two dollars for a pen unless it will also magically spring to life and write the Great American Novel for me while I sleep.

What's the value of a pen that (ultimately) cost two thousand dollars in my life which my daughter would probably drop into the toilet tomorrow? L. O. W.

Value is subjective, but that only serves to remind us that we're all unique snowflakes in the snow globe of life.

Needs vs. Wants

Another way you've heard this Think Wealthy point is in the classic Need vs. Want comparison.

Is the thing you're about to spend money on a NEED or a WANT? If you're in consumer debt, simply spend your money on fewer WANTS until you can afford them.

Here my mom has it right whenever I ask her for a Christmas list: "Honey, we're at an age where we don't NEED anything. Besides, that's just one less thing for me to dust!"

(I hate dusting, too.)

That thing you THINK you need may just be one more thing you have to dust – NOW what's the value in it?

Maybe I should change this Think Wealthy point from "Think Value First" to "Think Dust First."

◆　◆　◆

Wealth Tip: *Know Your 'No'*

Your money is your money. Unless you stole it in which case you suck and you can't hang out with us cool honest money people any longer.

Your money is your money. You worked hard for it. YOU decide where it goes and where it doesn't go.

How often does a kid selling something at your front door make you fork over your money even if you have no interest in it?

Here's a radical take – that graciously declining to buy whatever they're selling may be an even BETTER lesson for the little scampers in the end. (No, I'm not 80 years old, I don't know where the word 'scampers" came from. This may be the last time it's in print before it finally disappears from the English language.)

It seems like most people don't realize that their money is…well, THEIRS. And I'm not referring to people who say that it's all God's money, anyway. Of course, it's not really yours – you can't take it with you – but while you're here on Earth and not buried in it or scattered on top of it, it IS yours to decide *what* to do with, *when* you want to.

If you don't LOVE the new car or new house you're about to spend your hard-earned money on, DON'T do it.

If an investment doesn't feel right, DON'T do it.

"But so-and-so will think…" So-and-so can go fly a kite in thunderstorm. There's too much guilt surrounding money in these United States of ours.

What you do with your money is your business. You can ask others for advice – and certainly should from time to time, but you then take the advice, or you don't. And you stand behind the decision whether it proves to be weak or strong. No guilt.

To become wealthy, you have to develop your "no." Your resolute "no thanks" or "no, thank you" that will stop people in their tracks from trying to "convince" you to buy something you don't want or need or don't understand, whether it's a kid at the front door or the car salesperson with their list of upsells to run you through.

If you WANT the upsells, great! But if you don't, know your no. It's quiet and calm and can stop a bull running right at you in his tracks.

If the bull's first language is English.

Trust me. If you ever come into wealth quickly, people are going to come out of the woodwork asking for money (because everyone knows better than YOU how you should spend it...on THEM). And if you don't "Know Your No," it'll all be gone and those people will all vanish back into the foggy marshes from whence they crawled.

To the panhandler asking for a dollar if you're not feeling it: "Sorry, buddy."

To the neighborhood do-gooder seeking donations to protect the rights of unborn endangered mosquito larvae: "I appreciate your passion for the cause, but I'm not interested. If you ever switch sides and start selling bug lamps that ensure mosquitoes die a slow and painful death, I'll be your first sale, though!"

To that adorable, freckled and pig-tailed Girl Scout in front of the grocery store asking you to buy her troop's cookies: "Sorry, not today. But I'm sure you'll sell out real soon!"

You don't have to say yes to everyone who comes around asking for money. For YOUR money.

I have only recently felt comfortable with this thinking wealthy point myself.

Know your 'No.'

Know that you can say 'No' much more often than you realize.

Know that saying no doesn't make you an a-hole simply for saying 'No.' You might be perceived as one if you scream it at everyone but there's a very easy and polite way to do it.

"No, thank you" with a warm smile on your face.

That's all you need to say.

What we're aiming to do with this point is teach you to know the value of a dollar, more specifically the value of YOUR dollars, without having to justify anything to anyone else.

When you know your 'no' you'll also better know your OWN worth and not be afraid to let others know it, too. That's confidence, not ego, my friend. And that is the gift to yourself that will never stop paying dividends.

◆ ◆ ◆

Wealth Warning: *"We can't afford that"*

I heard that phrase so many times growing up that it was etched firmly into the growing folds of my grey matter.

I went out into the world thinking that very few of the things I wanted (even needed, sometimes) I could afford.

We need to shift the conversation to not purchasing something because you don't believe it's of VALUE enough for you at the time, not because you can't afford it.

It sounds like a small difference, but it's actually quite large because it involves you standing firm in making a financial decision.

Declaring that you don't see the VALUE of a purchase puts you in charge of what you do with your money as opposed to being a victim to the scarcity of dollar bills that (you think) exists in the world.

My partner Chris said a few years back, after coming back from the barber, that he loved his haircut so much that he wished he could get one twice a month, but that we couldn't afford that. Because I had been teaching myself to think wealthy I said, "Stop right there. Dude, we can AFFORD to do that – in fact," I pulled up the calculator on my phone, punched a few buttons and said, "you can have an extra haircut a month for the next 750 years if you want, but the real question is do you see the *value* in it?"

It might sound like a minor point to call out, but it's a disempowering mindset that we need to hear and catch as soon as it happens.

Before I had a certain level of financial security, I could always deflect a proposed vacation destination by friends – or going out to a local restaurant even – with the excuse that I couldn't afford it. "Maybe next year I can make it to Cabo." Or "Sure, if only I had a million dollars!"

Those are great reasons to give, or they sound like them. But what I later realized was what was really happening is that I was hiding behind my circumstances.

Now that we do have more means, we have to get to the root of what we do and don't want to spend our money on. Which is a much more powerful place to come from because we can't be swayed once we make a decision.

You can certainly say "it's not in our budget this month" or "this year" which communicates the same message just with you in the driver's seat now.

Don't use the fact that you can't afford something to mask the fact of whether it even holds enough value for you and your family. And don't use "we can't afford it" as an excuse against everything that your kids want because it will teach them that the world is full of lack and scarcity.

If you follow behind me while shopping *anywhere* with my daughter, you'll never hear me respond to her multiple requests to buy things, that we can't afford them. "No, honey, we're not getting that today" or "I don't see the value in that" are my go-to lines and that's that.

If the wealthy genuinely can't afford something that they want badly enough, they figure out how *to* afford it and they go do it.

◆ ◆ ◆

Wealth Warning: *"That's How They Getcha!"*

This ties in closely with a money belief I was raised with that everyone is out to get your money. How often did you grow up hearing, "That's where they getcha!" Or "That's how they getcha!"

I'm guilty of this as much as the next feller or lady, but so often we think of a purchase we're about to make as being pure profit going into the immediate business owner's pocket. We get indignant about it, that "they just want to separate me from my cash!" but we forget that every business has its fair share of bills and taxes to pay, too.

"These prices are highway robbery!" we say without knowing anything about the company's financial obligations.

The idea behind this is that you've been duped or *had* by a company that was just trying to profit off you.

Every company may be trying to get into my wallet, but it's my wallet and I'll let in whoever provides the most value back to me.

But it's not a fight. It's just a company or someone selling a product or service for x number of dollars and I get to decide whether it's worth it or not.

It's your money. Leave the emotion out of it and simply determine whether it's of value to you. Or not.

◆ ◆ ◆

Wealth Warning: *Loaning money to family and friends.*

There are those people in the world who give their money away to family and friends and those who don't. I'm always surprised to hear a friend tell me that so-and-so owes them $1,000 but they don't think they'll ever get it back.

OF COURSE YOU WON'T.

(Probably.)

If you want to keep the friendship, don't ask for it back. The damage is often already done, though, if the ATM at the Friendship Bank (you!) has opened for business.

I don't think I've ever had a friend ask me for money. And I don't think it's because I've appeared more financially broke than them – though maybe I've looked like it at times. (Have I mentioned how much I *hate* clothes shopping? And that I have a T-shirt that is 20 years old?)

Maybe it's the energy I've given off. I've also never asked anyone to loan me money in a tough spot. (Except for banks in the form of credit cards – and boy did I ask them for "loans" over the years.)

My bottom line is that if you loan money to family or friends, you best never expect it back, so you don't end up resenting whoever hasn't paid it back and who then starts avoiding you.

If you give money away to friends and family without an acknowledgement of any terms and conditions (even if the terms are that you don't expect it back), you may very quickly turn into an ATM in their eyes.

THINK WEALTHY #4: THINK OF WHAT'S POSSIBLE

With anything and everything in your life, there is the current reality and the future possibility.

Today is what today is and tomorrow is what tomorrow will be.

What most of us do, however, is meld together our current reality and future possibility as if they are one and the same. Yesterday and today have already convinced you that tomorrow is going to be just another helping of what was served on your lunch tray today, right?

We subtract out the possibility of what tomorrow COULD be because we're in a rut or we're scared of change or we have no goals in place…or because we're just plain hopeless and depressed, even.

Or we're just comfortable where we are… simple inertia!

When you start to think of what's possible – and think that way consistently – your entire view of the world changes. In fact, YOUR world changes.

Your imagination is now engaged in problem-solving. You've activated your creativity and the juices are flowing.

You also feel in control because you're taking a stand that things can be better than they are right now. There is hope. Not that today isn't the crappiest day of your life, but can't tomorrow always be a day of new experiences, connections and joy?

The very fact that you start looking at the world through the lens of possibility means that you see the potential in your own capabilities, too.

You see the potential in yourself.

And if you're seeing the potential in yourself, you'll see the potential in others as well.

When you see what's POSSIBLE in the world life suddenly…comes alive!

The biggest result of this is that you stop complaining about whatever is or isn't happening in your life right now. When you learn to think in terms of what's possible, what just IS right now becomes the fuel you need for tomorrow's accomplishments.

How many years of our lives do we spend looking at a situation or state of affairs and complaining to ourselves and others that it shouldn't be that way?

YEARS!

My grandma shouldn't have died when I was five – I never got to know her.

Why was this POTUS elected? He or she is ruining this country! If they're re-elected…I'm moving to Canada…I swear…but I *mean* it this time!

I'm thirty years old, single and still in massive student loan debt while other friends have families and beautiful homes in the suburbs – why is MY life so hard?

When you complain and live from what's not possible, you FEEL like a victim because your perceived problems make you feel small and powerless.

When you look at the world from what IS possible, your brain gets a zap of electricity like the shock that brought Frankenstein to life.

(Okay, maybe not quite that big of a shock.)

For anyone who has ever created something, it all started with an idea in their head. This can be anything from the creation of an otherworldly literary character like Harry Potter to a completely new innovation or invention such as the Snuggie or iPhone.

How do you know if you're not living in what's possible?

Figure out how much time you spend complaining about the state of your life or listening to others moan about their lives and validating them.

It might surprise you.

Today is only today.

Tomorrow is what you create it to be.

◆ ◆ ◆

Wealth Secret: *Positive people run the world.*

The world is not run by people who think negatively.

The world is not run by people who are hopeless about humanity's ability to change its lot in life.

The world is run by people who believe in a better future and who can share and communicate that vision to others.

The true leaders of our governments and our corporations, of our school systems, they are motivated by a future full of possibilities. They speak in the language of possibility.

You are the leader of your life.

To see what's possible, you need a mindset that is bathed in positive thought. Positive thinking is the backbone of creativity – it's jet fuel for your imagination.

Negative thinking, on the other hand, destroys.

Negative thinking destroys ideas, it destroys morale…it single-handedly stops progress dead in its tracks.

Good leaders, by definition, are positive, future-facing people who consciously steer their minds to what's possible for themselves and others – they don't focus on obstacles.

You would be hard-pressed to find a CEO of any quality that isn't painting a picture of the best of what's ahead for the company as opposed to obsessing about what there is to overcome on the way to that goal.

Are you living in a space of what's possible or are you stuck in a victim mentality where life is a constant struggle?

This should come as no surprise that of the two outlooks on life, positive people are the successful ones.

They are also the much wealthier ones (financially and emotionally) because they see opportunities, engage and inspire others, create their own luck and make things happen.

◆ ◆ ◆

Wealth Tip: *See opportunity everywhere you look.*

The only constant in the world is change.

People are born, a litter of puppies pops out of dog bits, flowers bloom…life happens in all its amazing variation and then – spoiler alert – everything dies.

Life is nothing if not CHANGE.

In fact, change is the only thing you can count on. Turns out Buddha was onto something over 2,500 years ago when he said that change was not the problem, it is only RESISTANCE to change that causes suffering.

The catch here is that we're not hardwired to like or accept change – we're not programmed for it. Our amazing, sexy brains are constantly scanning for patterns in our environments to give us the illusion of order and stability.

Your entire life is supported by what you perceive as pillars of unchanging truths.

But, ultimately, life is change.

With that acknowledgment, here's a secret that wealthy people know:

With change there is opportunity.

A wealthy mindset welcomes change.

Change means that value is shifting and there is a void where something shiny and new will be ready to provide the value others want or need.

Change?

YAY!!!

So how do we learn to see opportunity?

First, we need to tune our radar for hearing any pain points people have. Where is someone complaining about a product or service?

All those people who are negative about the world and can't wait to tell you about it – they may just be your best idea generators! I wouldn't hang out with them for long since negative cooties are easily caught, but any time you spend time with a negative person, think of them as brainstormers of your future wealth.

And thank them all the way to the IPO of your company. When you're standing on the floor of the New York Stock Exchange to ring the opening bell, you can publicly thank Bernie in accounting for bitching all day, every day, to you five years ago about his whatchamacallit that you built a company around.

I used to scan the Wall Street Journal that was delivered to my house each day (a "free" subscription from award miles on an airline I no longer flew) and I would see nothing but opportunity for creating better mousetraps for people. That doesn't mean that I'm passionate about any of those areas of opportunity, but I saw them right before my eyes.

Wherever there is a pain point for one person, there is opportunity. The more people who share the pain point, the more financial opportunity that exists.

Opportunities create wealth for those who see and seize them.

Embrace change as the gift it is for wherever there is change, there is opportunity.

It'll also make your life easier as you step into acceptance and flow of the world around you.

◆ ◆ ◆

Wealthy Tip*: Always Be Learning*

Only the smartest people know that they know nothing.

In terms of intellect and formal education, the reality is that each of us only knows the tiniest of slivers about our particular fields of interest.

Yet the world is a FASCINATING place – if you're willing to admit that you don't know much about it.

I was watching a profile of Bill Gates on 60 Minutes and my jaw dropped when Charlie Rose took their cameras inside Bill's (you know, we're tight like that) private office – and there on the shelf were dozens and dozens of The Great Courses DVDs.

First off, I have ordered a few of those myself so I was comforted to learn I'll soon be wrestling Bill Gates for his on-again, off-again world's wealthiest man title.

Second of all, it was only a few years ago that I would've thought that someone as wealthy as Bill Gates had a pretty good handle on how much book knowledge he has or needs in his life.

Nope, turns out he understands the power of interdisciplinary thought, how learning about one area can benefit a completely different area, and he knows how to stay CURIOUS and, therefore, stay CREATIVE as he and his (now ex) wife go about giving away billions of dollars toward causes they care about and are working to change.

That 60 Minutes segment was all the proof I needed that some of the wealthiest people are always learning, always asking questions, staying creative and nimble, always wanting to know how they can help others and improve the world around them. He also had a tote bag of books he was at various stages of reading…say what?!?

Think about the sharks on Shark Tank – they are always listening and learning from the people they meet on the show.

They might know the trends of their own industries pretty well, but they don't know anything about how to make beer-flavored ice cream or how large the market for it is.

Always be thinking, "What can I learn from every person I meet?"

Everyone knows something that you don't. Together you might find amazing synergy for your next project or business opportunity. Or perhaps you'll just be able to file away a little piece of information that will help someone else out.

Lest we not forget that the biggest wealth-building tool of all is your BRAIN.

◆ ◆ ◆

Wealth Tip: *Embrace obstacles…they ain't going anywhere.*

Of course you're going to have obstacles.

Everyone has them, including children of super-wealthy parents.

We all have obstacles because life is unpredictable.

But we also *need* them in our lives. Without obstacles, there is no growth. And without growth, life would be pretty darn boring.

Anyone who has met with success wouldn't trade in all the failures that preceded their success because they know the value of those lessons along the way.

Let others help you when you're stuck – doesn't it feel good to help other people when the shoe's on the other foot?

THINK WEALTHY #5:
THINK BIG

No. Bigger!

What you are able to achieve in this world is only limited by your imagination.

However big of a life you want to live, I want you to dream even bigger!

I'm talking about dreaming with a plan of action to put behind it, of course, not The Secret dreaming where you fall asleep every night hugging your tear-soaked vision board wondering where your buxom supermodel wife is or why Hugh Jackman hasn't left his wife for you yet because yes, that's what would REALLY make your life complete.

One of the biggest obstacles people have on the road to well-rounded wealth is the limit of their own imaginations – instead of dreaming you have a million dollars in the bank, envision ten million or fifty million. I guarantee that when you know you DESERVE it, your brain will get creative on ways of how to bring it to your door.

What you are capable of is only limited by your imagination. I don't care if you're 18 or 80, you have plenty of time left to make a difference in the world.

And you're not going to run out of energy because you'll be passionate about what you're doing and that is its own internal power plant.

◆ ◆ ◆

Wealth Tip: *The world is soooooooooooooooo big.*

The world is much bigger than you can ever understand.

Given the phenomenal diversity of human beings, anytime you think you have life figured out, stop and remember that the overwhelming majority of people in the world DON'T think like you. Heck, your neighbors on all sides don't think like you.

Any time I was dreading going into the office of past employment, I would drive past businesses on the morning commute and think how many hundreds of people worked in all those buildings that I drove past, jobs that were not the one that I was headed into (and not liking) and I would dream that they actually enjoyed what they did and were fulfilled by them.

Just thinking about the phenomenal diversity of jobs and careers in my tiny five-mile commute into the office popped me out of my head and my "woe is me" mentality – it reignited and excited me about how big the world is and that there must be HUNDREDS of jobs out there that were a better fit for me than the current one – I just needed to find it.

To stop and periodically try to grasp the enormity of the world and the vast difference in experiences that people have had should help you see your own problems in a different light, too – it should shrink them down so that YOU, that endless potential you are in each new moment, can become bigger than all your perceived problems pooled together.

You are a gazillion times bigger than your problems. (And that's a lot, as my 7-year-old will tell you.)

All you have to do is watch other people overcome unfathomable odds and circumstances to achieve their goals and you'll soon realize that you have everything within you to do the same.

◆ ◆ ◆

Wealth Tip: *Commit to being wealthy.*

Now that you are thinking and dreaming big and that you can overcome any obstacle that stands in your way, what we need is a fire in the belly, the commitment to make a plan for success and to then follow it, one step at a time.

Know you're WORTHY of wealth like people who are wealthy do as we saw in Book 2, *Understand Wealth*.

You have every chance of becoming wealthy if you want to.

Most people are ashamed to admit that they want to be wealthy. Money is "bad" or wealthy people are thought to be amoral or greedy or ruthless – whatever the reason, most people WANT to have more money, but they don't want to ADMIT it out loud. Therefore, they don't commit to DOING anything about it because it signifies a break with the herd mentality of the middle class.

Even if you live in BFE, America and for you to leave $100,000 to your heirs when you die is wealth, commit to it!

Done. And kudos to you in advance!

Make a promise to yourself – do it for your kids, find whatever motivates you to embrace the planning and the work ahead and DO IT.

If money is bad or a taboo topic, go back to the first page of the first book, _Understand Money_, and work your way back here. I'll wait.

[whistling the Muppet Show theme]

Good…moving right along!

THINK WEALTHY #6: THINK "WHY NOT ME?"

The only thing that keeps us from enjoying life and accepting any good fortune that we create for ourselves or that comes our way is our own limited thinking. It stems from a belief that we don't DESERVE the good that we're experiencing or receiving.

How often have you heard people say that they became nervous or scared when things were going "too well for them" in their lives as if the universe always must balance out any good fortune you're experiencing with misfortune?

It doesn't. The universe does not need to balance out you feeling good with you feeling bad.

The underlying belief a person holds here is, "I don't deserve to be this happy or feel this good or this fortunate."

You've probably even thought this yourself at one point, that "all good things must come to an end" or that you don't want to "push your luck" or, God forbid, get used to "too much of a good thing."

That doesn't sound like the self-talk of someone who creates their own life and knows that, if they dream it, they can achieve it, does it?

It stems from thinking that the world is us vs. them where there's a group of people who are lucky or wealthy or happy all the time and who deserve IT ALL…and then there's the rest of us.

So. Many. People. Do. This.

We feel on some cellular level that we don't deserve good fortune or happiness for more than a few fleeting moments.

My partner and I used to think this way and now we stop it dead in its tracks. And you can, too!

For years now as Chris and I have been invited to exclusive charity events where paddles are flying into the air for $100,000 or even $500,000 donations or to dinner parties with friends who live in beautiful mansions in the Hollywood Hills or invited out on yachts to sail the waters off of the coast of Los Angeles – whenever we find ourselves in a situation where someone from the outside looking in would think we may very well be wealthy just for being in that environment, one of us will turn to the other and say, "Why NOT us?"

Indeed, why not us?

Why not us to just enjoy this day or night or weekend?

The only thing that would keep us from enjoying life at that level is our own set of limiting beliefs – or guilt – that we were somehow unworthy of having the experience, that we were fooling everyone into thinking that we belonged there, that we were not inherently interesting or smart enough to fit in – whatever the limiting belief is.

Every wealthy person has already made that mental leap at some point in their lives to just accept wherever they are.

So why not us?

There is no reason why not us.

And why not YOU?

There is no reason why not YOU.

None.

When good things happen to you or money falls into your lap or you're gifted something that you've always wanted, stop, say "thank you" and think to yourself, "Of course! Why *not* me?"

It's that simple.

◆ ◆ ◆

Wealth Tip: *"Yes, Please!"*

For years whenever I would receive a check for *whatever* work I had done, I would stare down at the check and sigh, shoulders slumped carrying the weight of the world because I knew it already had been spent before I'd even cashed it.

That's what debt does to you. After all, where is the joy in making ANY amount of money when it is "already spent."

Or so it felt. Having left college with a liberal arts degree double major in Linguistics and French (those direct paths to money-printing) and $50,000 of student loans – all I'd known as an adult was deep debt and no clear career path to paying it off.

I had to consciously change my attitude toward money by realizing that any income was MY money to decide what to do with – in that light I started treating every check I received as if it were my new best friend.

I had to become a good RECEIVER – of money, of compliments, of whatever.

I had to consciously reprogram my mind to love money and to respect any money that was coming into my life.

Consciously changing from the thought that I worked only to pay down my debt to the fact that I was in CONTROL of my life and OPEN to money flowing to and through me allowed me to open my eyes and ears to other opportunities where I could earn even more money. It took that literal behavior modification on my part to change the thought process and underlying belief behind it.

By consciously CHOOSING what I wanted to do with my money, I was no longer a victim to my debt or to my life's circumstances, in general.

It's a trap I still fall into sometimes, but by and large, with every check I receive, no matter how small, I get excited as if I had just won it big in Vegas.

A $2 rebate check for paper at Staples? "Awe! Some!"

Annual residuals check of $15 for an episode of Unsolved Mysteries that I shot over 20 years ago? "Bring it on, bitches!"

Sidenote: Those tiny residual checks rolling in each year actually vested me into the SAG/AFTRA pension plan so now when I retire, not only will I have our savings, tax-advantaged retirement accounts and Social Security, but I'll also have a boost of a pension that will only grow larger and larger if I ever do more work under that union's contracts.

"Would you like more money, Todd?!?"

Yes, please!

"Would you like bigger life experiences and meeting new people to find your next opportunities where you can provide value back to the world?"

Yes, please!

This is about saying YES to life, in general, as you never know where your next great idea or opportunity is going to come from, but it will most definitely come from meeting and sharing ideas with other people.

◆ ◆ ◆

Wealth Tip: *Imagine yourself in any situation.*

Anytime you think of the life you'd like to lead, whether by seeing other people on TV or reading about them, immediately put yourself in that position.

If you see a beautiful house in Malibu with infinite views of the Pacific Ocean, think about that being YOUR house.

What happens next? Does your chest tighten from fear of living there and everything that comes along with that? Or does it all flow?

Is the house so big that it has any live-in staff there just to maintain it? Who are they and how do you interact with them?

You can imagine yourself into any situation – and if you don't like how you respond in your imagination, you can start working on that right now. As part of our Be – Do – Have equation from Book 3, *Meet Your Inner Billionaire*, BE the person who can HAVE that life first, so it has a chance of becoming a reality.

◆ ◆ ◆

Wealth Tip: *10M dollars – right now!*

Stop what you're doing – well, keep reading the book – but stop thinking of everything you need to get done or that funny cat video you're about to watch on your phone and imagine that you have $10,000,000 just sitting in a host of bank accounts right now.

You have a net worth in cash (meaning in checking or savings accounts, liquid and not invested) of $10,000,000.

How do you feel? Did you just take a deep breath in and exhale for the 1st time in a long time because you've spent your life buried under consumer debt? Some people tear up when they really commit to this exercise.

What would you do first – pay off all your debt?

Sure, you'd want to pay off any consumer debt that has kept you on the hamster wheel for all these years, but you'd want to consult with your CPA before paying off your mortgage to make sure that a little debt on the books isn't a good thing tax-wise.

But once you're out of debt, then what happens – what do you do next?

Let's say you spend a million to get the house you want, upgrade your wardrobe and all of that. Now what?

Isn't your life still the life you have right now? You may have more things, but when you have enough money to do anything you want, what do you do?

Sometimes I say to Chris while we're out on a date night to imagine we have 10 million in the bank right now – what would change about our life and our lifestyle? And it's always surprisingly little.

We'd be more generous with holiday trips to see family and we'd plan more vacation travel, but we don't feel we NEED much more than we have right now so anything beyond what we NEED for a secure retirement is just money to be invested in businesses we believe in (our own or someone else's) and shared with causes and charities that resonate with us.

And, of course, we might stop ordering off the right-side of the restaurant menu where the prices are listed – HOORAY, fewer chicken entrees in our future!

What about you? You have 10 million dollars staring back at you from your banking app – how do you feel and what do you do?

◆ ◆ ◆

Wealth Warning: *The Pedestal Effect*

This will either apply to you outright or you won't have any idea what the heck I'm talking about, but this has been a biggie for me.

I always used to put rich people on a pedestal – because my family did. Although my parents always wanted to have more money, they also idealized the idea of being rich and what it must be like to have a great amount of financial breathing room.

My mom would start dragging out her syllables when talking about people that appeared richer than her. Just the fact that they had more than us was enough to get our respect and admiration.

"Did you seeeeee the way they decorated their hoooouuuuuse? Oh my gooooooodness! We would just never THINK to do ANY of that!"

"Mom, you know the Stronzi family come from a long line of mafioso connections, right?"

"Every party has a pooper, Todd! Now go to bed so the Tooth Fairy can leave you an I.O.U. until your father hits the Powerball."

It's as if anyone who was wealthy was cut from a different cloth. They were not people that we would casually hang out with – they ran in different circles and left a trail of hundred-dollar bills in their path from their overflowing pockets.

Unbeknownst to me, I inherited this belief about how different rich and wealthy people were, from you and me.

As I mentioned in the introduction, living in Los Angeles and projecting 35mm films years ago in the super-posh homes in the wealthiest parts of town, I'd peek out of the porthole, watching "those rich people" rearrange pillows in their private screening rooms, trying to catch a glimpse of how different and more refined and mannered they MUST be – if I could just learn and mimic their wealthy way of fluffing a pillow, it would immediately start beefing up my own bank account.

I was trying to figure out the secrets to their success by observing their behavior so I could become just like them.

The problem with that outlook is I'd constructed a mental wall between who I am and who they are as if the wealthy are a monochromatic group of people operating under one set of rules (which includes the proper way to fluff a couch pillow, apparently) that remains elusive to the rest of us.

When, in fact, they are just people who saw opportunities, perhaps took big risks, who invested in themselves and knew what to do with the money when it came in.

They knew to earn more than they spend and invest the rest – dam it!

The pedestal effect is just more Us vs. Them thinking that I have encountered more than a few times in my life.

Now I'd rather know HOW they made and maintain their wealth – there may be things I could learn from their journeys, but not from how they arranged the pillows on their couches or tossed peanut M&M's into their mouths while I started up the film in the projection booth behind them.

The bottom line is to not put people on a pedestal – it means you're looking UP for wisdom and which requires them to look DOWN to share it – and everyone just ends up with pains and sprains in their necks.

The difference between a wealthy person's net worth and yours is often just a punctuation mark or two.

What you can learn from them, however, is invaluable. And vice-versa.

See everyone as a peer and you'll be more yourself – more genuine and unguarded – your authenticity will shine through which is what matters most.

You are not in competition with people who are wealthy – you are fellow travelers along the same road looking out for each other and helping each other along. The wealthy are really only in competition with themselves, just as YOU are only really in competition with YOUR self.

THINK WEALTHY #7:
THINK OF
YOURSELF AS CEO
OF YOU, INC.

No one is going to take better care of your life than you are.

It was your parents' job to make sure you were safe, dry-diapered and fed on time, but at some point, you get to run your own life. You probably kicked and screamed through puberty and adolescence for your freedom – now here we are – you wanted it you, you got it!

Congrats on the promotion!

You are the CEO of You, Inc. and that has never been more apparent than in this corporation-agnostic, job-hopping, LinkedIn-orgy-of-career-whoredom that we're currently in.

Just as no one is going to take better care of you than YOU, no one is going to take better care of your MONEY than you are. People may ADVISE you on what to do with your money – and at some point, you should let them – but never let go of the reins.

So let's get down to the very important business of You, Inc.

How are the company's financials? Is it healthy, in general? Will it be around in ten years based on current spending? Does the company have all of its risks mitigated via insurance and wills and trusts to ensure as smooth of sailing as possible?

As CEO, how is your integrity – would you want to do business with YOU? Would you trust you in a negotiation? Do you trust you to show up at a meeting on time and prepared or will you just wing it and barely squeak by? Do you have a vision for the company to help steer it through the exciting, unknown waters of the future? Or are you fixating on the company's past performance, the good, the bad and the ugly?

But hey, you're freakin' CEO now. Whatever you don't like, change it!

No big deal. Companies pivot all the time.

It's very important that you not be critical of the job you're doing as CEO – forgive yourself and move on.

When you know better, you do better.

And as CEOs, we're ALL working to improve ourselves which, in turn, will improve company morale and ensure that we are running a solid business from the CEO on down.

Do you see what's happening as you internalize all of these Think Wealthy points?

You're becoming the real leader of your own life.

You always have been, but now you're actually starting to believe it.

❖ ❖ ❖

Wealth Tip: *Pursue Profits, Not Wages*

Wealthy people invest in themselves because they believe in themselves.

They know that whatever they don't know they can learn from someone else or pay someone else to do, so they take chances.

Think of a salesman who doesn't believe in his abilities and so he chooses a salary with a base of $80,000 and a commission of 5% on all sales. If he has a million in sales for the year, he'll make $130,000 ($80,000 base + $50,000 in commissions).

Contrast that with a person who Thinks Wealthy and who negotiates a base salary of $40,000 but a commission structure of 30% on all sales. On that same million in sales for the company as the previous example, they'll take home $340,000 ($40,000 base + $300,000 in commissions). That's over twice as much as our friend who doesn't believe in his abilities.

This is a fabricated example as a 30% sales commission is quite high and it must be a product or service with incredible margins like a subscription model or SAAS, but I'm using it to prove a point.

Someone who invests in THEMSELVES is believing 100% in their own ability to drive sales and bring home the bacon.

They create businesses because they believe they can deliver great value to the marketplace and be well-compensated for it.

In general, people who Think Wealthy seek (or create) opportunities where they can make more money than they would with a flat pay structure. They incentivize themselves to work harder and smarter and deliver on their objectives, be they for another company or for their own.

They have a self-confidence that makes them see and accept the opportunities that come their way.

I'll keep hammering away at this until the cows come home because it took me that long to get it.

Wealthy people invest in themselves. They align their compensation with their performance because they know a share of the profits is a much stronger incentive than an hourly wage which, ultimately, puts a cap on what they can earn.

Work for profits and the sky is the limit. Work for hourly wages and you are capped by time to the total income you can earn.

If your compensation isn't linked to a company's profits or earnings, you will always be trading time for money. And there are only so many hours in a day.

MOO.

◆ ◆ ◆

Wealth Tip: Would you hire you?

As the CEO of You, Inc. your decisions affect the fate of the entire company. If you were to meet you in an interview, does the candidate (you!) seem confident in their abilities? Do you trust them (you!)?

Heck, do you even LIKE them (you!)?

In the real world, for any job that you're going after, put yourself in the interviewer's seat – what qualities in the candidate sitting across from you will make *your* job SO MUCH easier? The secret is that everyone is looking to hire someone who makes their job that much easier, from your immediate supervisor all the way up to the CEO.

You want the next hire to be the home run for the company.

Be the home run. And, for the love of butter, don't beat yourself if you don't get a second interview. How people do or don't see you is dependent on a million factors, but one of them is never your own underlying worth as a human being.

Bottom line is would you want to hire you in your position? If not, become that person – become the person that sets the bar high and delivers on those goals.

◆ ◆ ◆

Wealth Tip*: Share your vision of the future.*

Share your vision of the future you want for yourself and others to live into.

Life is a team sport. If you have a vision for your own life that you can passionately share with others, you will inspire them.

This is what the best leaders do in their personal or professional lives – they share their bold vision of a better world and the force of their conviction pulls others in line with it and everyone sets about making it come true. Everyone wants to live in that new world, too!

What do you want for your life? Why not envision it, share it and then create it? No one else will do it for you.

◆ ◆ ◆

Wealth Tip: *Compete with yourself – and love the competition.*

As soon as I say to compete with yourself, a whole chorus of people will chime in and say they do and that when they don't succeed at something, they beat themselves up unmercifully just like they're supposed to.

And they'll say that with a hint of pride, the beating-themselves-up part.

"I mean, I'm just too much of a perfectionist, Todd. It's got to be the best or I'm not happy."

To which I reply, "That's very fascinating, annoying person who reminds me of my former self!"

There's a difference between doing the best job you can and basing your self-worth on your performance.

You are an amazingly complex individual – give yourself a break and do really great work. Save the perfect work for brain surgery on me if I need it (and if you're a brain surgeon). Otherwise, what daily perfectionism does is make you a martyr and a blowhard and most people see right through it.

When I say to compete with yourself, I'm talking about doing the things you want and need to do, striving for wealth, for freedom, for safety, because you are your only REAL competition.

No one is going to know if you did the best job possible except for you.

So do your best work. Always. Because you are your own best benchmark for how you're doing in life.

And if you didn't do your best, ask yourself why, tweak something and move on.

Every time you compare yourself with someone else, you put one person higher than the other and you either judge yourself against them or you judge them against you and that stops the baseball game of life mid-pitch.

When you look around and only see people higher or lower than you, you don't have any peers. Yet the secret is that everyone's a peer when you're confident in who you are.

◆ ◆ ◆

Wealth Tip: *Do what you say.*

Do what you say you're going to do.

If you don't do what you say, no one will trust you. They will lose faith in you and that takes a long time to rebuild.

This one sounds easier than it is in practice.

Be a person of your word – you will stand out among your peers. Guaranteed.

If you say you'll follow up on Tuesday, follow up on Tuesday. Set a reminder – you may need a system in place to help you keep your word.

If you know you can't make it to a lunch appointment, cancel it as soon as you can, not an hour beforehand – it shows respect for the other person's time.

That's all keeping your word does – it elicits the highest trust and respect from others. It also shows others that you value THEIR time. Which you do because you know the value of your OWN time.

One side effect of this is that you stop being passive-aggressive. You "know your no" so you end up not having to spend any of your time playing games in order to get your real feelings across.

And if your time is important, so is everyone else's – it's all the same. And if someone doesn't realize their time is important yet, you can lead by example.

You know you're dealing with a class act when someone much wealthier or more powerful than you doesn't keep you waiting.

Do what you say.

◆ ◆ ◆

Wealth Tip: Don't be the smartest person in the room.

Or don't NEED to be, at least.

No one likes competing for honors. You're already CEO – it's your birthright. Relax and ask questions of people who know more, but YOU then make the decision. And stand behind it.

The wealthiest people consistently and deliberately hire and surround themselves with people who are smarter than them. This is why they're wealthy.

Period.

THINK WEALTHY #8:
THINK THANKS

Wealth starts with 'We.'

Always think thanks and GIVE thanks whenever you can.

I honestly thank you for reading this far into this book. No joke, many people won't get this far so you are part of a very select few and I am sincerely grateful that you have decided to spend this much time with me and my goofy humor as it relates to money and life.

Thank you!

See how easy that is? It feels good, too!

I challenge you to show me one wealthy person who did it all alone, who needed absolutely no one's help to reach the heights of their fame and financial glory.

It's an impossible challenge because no one does it all alone, regardless of what the media say.

And winning people over because you're such an awesome and inspiring person starts with gratitude for other people sharing their time and energy with you.

I can't say it enough…

No one becomes wealthy without the help of others. No one.

People, your family, your relationships – they are all assets, not liabilities.

Wealth starts with 'we.'

We have this lone wolf idea in our minds, this idea that people who become exceedingly wealthy are operating all alone in the world as if a company of one could amass millions of dollars in value – at minimum there are clients or customers that you need to think thanks for!

Facebook is a company of over 45,000 employees. You often only see Mark

Zuckerberg as the singular – face (Face?) – of the company, but dude is not doing it all alone. No one does.

Wealth starts with 'we.'

Life is a team sport and everyone's time is valuable so be sure to thank them for their help at every step of the way.

◆ ◆ ◆

Wealth Tip: *Gift and share randomly.*

Gift things to people because you want to, not to get something back.

Have you ever gifted something to someone anonymously and been able to see their eyes light up or see them break down in tears because they're in shock at the level of thought and generosity?

It's phenomenal. And you can do it at any time you like.

It's one of the greatest joys in life.

It doesn't have to be anonymous if we're talking between friends and it also doesn't need to be that extreme, but why not periodically send your favorite book to a handful of friends who might like it? Or send a bottle of your favorite wine to a new work buddy? Or randomly take a box of donuts or other treats into the office to kick off or end the workweek?

Everyone loves gracious surprises like these – why should we wait until holiday season each year to revel in the surprise and joy on others' faces?

There are so many ways to show gratitude and be thankful for the people who are in your life, past and present.

It feels great to give.

And that is REALLY the point of creating more wealth for you and your family than you ever could have imagined.

You're going to have to get really good at giving your money away so why not start now with small gifts to those you care about and work with?

Write one email a week to a different person thanking them and letting them know what you've learned from them. In one year you'll have 52 people who will do ANYTHING they can to help you out, too.

◆ ◆ ◆

Wealth Tip: *Learn people's names.*

I. Still. Suck. At. This.

But I'm getting better.

One of the easiest ways for people to remember YOU is for you to remember THEIR NAME in a five-minute conversation.

It shows you're attentive and that you care about that person, whether you'll ever see them again or not.

It's part of being charismatic.

There is a friend of a friend who used to own famous soundstages out here in Los Angeles. I probably met him ten different times over a couple of years and every single time we were introduced, he acted as if he had never met me before. Distant and disinterested were the words I might use to describe his body language.

It used to infuriate me that he would never remember that we had met before, never mind the fact that he couldn't squeak out my name even if he were being waterboarded.

It made me despise him. If someone mentioned his name, I'd roll my eyes.

This is an extreme case and it shows my pettier side, but we all have these people in our lives. If he had ever said, "I'm sorry, I know we've met, but I'm horrible with names"…that's one thing.

But to say nothing over the years means that I will gleefully dance on his grave when the Dark Lord of the Underworld comes to retrieve him.

Work hard to remember people's names. Or be gracious enough to admit that you're not good with them.

A trick I've found is to drop a person's name in at the end of a conversation – it will help you to cement their name even more in your mind and it will give their brain stem a little tickle of fondness for you.

And maybe, just maybe, they won't gleefully anticipate your demise at the hands of the Dark Lord of the Underworld, too.

THINK WEALTHY #9:
THINK "I GOT THIS!"

Fear will never go away.

And it shouldn't – fear keeps you on your toes and is a loyal talent scout for your hunches and intuition. Treat fear like a babbling toddler – listen to it to see if there's anything of value in its ramblings and then send it on its way.

Life is not supposed to come with an instruction guide. If it did, it would be immeasurably dull and predictable.

On whatever path you now tread and, in the future, think (and know), "I got this!"

You can figure out whatever needs to be figured out by yourself over time or with the help of others because – you got this!

Everything else is noise that can easily distract you from letting your true light and purpose shine out into the world.

◆ ◆ ◆

Wealth Tip: *You are bigger than your problems.*

You will have obstacles on the road of life from your first breath to your last. We all will. Even people with more money in the bank than you have them, too.

Problems, obstacles, hurdles, whatever you want to call them, are there for a reason and all you need to remember at the end of the day is that you are not the problem itself and you are not defined by the problem – you are infinitely bigger than the problem.

I'm repeating this point because it bears repeating – we too often associate our worth with the current obstacles staring us in the face.

◆ ◆ ◆

Wealth Tip: *See everyone as a survivor. Like you.*

Think of everyone you see out in the world – everyone you previously judged and gossiped about – they're all survivors the same as you.

And they're using all the tricks and potions and voodoo up their sleeve to stay safe in the game of life the same as you – that is how we're all much more alike than we are different.

You're a survivor and you do what you do because it worked for you in the past the same as others do today what has worked for them in the past.

Sympathy and empathy for your fellow man will never go out of style. And if it does…run!

◆ ◆ ◆

Wealth Tip: *Forgive yourself.*

Forgive yourself for not having done the ten things you didn't do yet today that would have ensured your success, or for not knowing what your net worth is to the decimal point or how much consumer debt you have.

Forgive yourself and just snicker at the goofy things you do and have done along your journey up to this point, to you reading this sentence right now.

I'm not sure if guilt is the gift that keeps on giving in America from our Mayflower ancestors, but it's time we all stop beating ourselves up.

Forgive yourself.

You are enough.

After you reach adulthood, it's no one's job to tell you this any longer.

Just as you were yesterday, just as you are today and just as you will be tomorrow.

Forgive yourself – you are enough.

THINK WEALTHY #10: STOP THINKING AND DO

You are awesome.

Have I mentioned that already?

You have read through all of these points and your brain is on fire as new pathways are created for you to Think Wealthy.

That's all great and wonderful and stupendous, but unless you take ACTION toward a goal, no matter how small, and follow it up with another small step, and another, then this is all a big, hot steaming feel-good cup of mental doodoo.

The theory behind this book on how to Think Wealthy is that your thoughts will motivate you to take action, your thoughts will actually PULL you into the habits that will reward you in the form of financial wealth due to all the value you will be providing to the world.

That's how it works – in theory.

So, for the love of all that is sacred and holy and blessed with the color green and that smells like sweet, sweet cash, PLEASE stop thinking and go DO something to start on the path to your dreams. And then do one more step. And another and another…

Wealthy people act quickly. It's just a muscle like any other that they've trained. They're used to being proactive to a newfound opportunity.

Ethical, wealthy people do what they say they're going to do, and they explore every opportunity with vim and vigor until they know whether it has the potential to be a winner – or they discover it's a dud and they go back to their regular routine of seeing other opportunities and kicking ass.

We have spent the first four books in this personal finance series working on the internal side of the wealthier you – we have been working on the BE side of our BE – DO – HAVE equation because that is the foundation for all the actions you will DO in your life to HAVE the life of your dreams.

Per this Think Wealthy point #10, however, now it is time to infuse our actions with the underlying beliefs of our inner billionaire and tackle the DO part of the equation.

Action is SO IMPORTANT I'm going to stop this point right–